hrjc

ALEX OVECHKIN

Published by ABDO Publishing Company, 8000 West 78th Street, Edina, Minnesota 55439. Copyright © 2011 by Abdo Consulting Group, Inc. International copyrights reserved in all countries. No part of this book may be reproduced in any form without written permission from the publisher. SportsZone™ is a trademark and logo of ABDO Publishing Company.

Printed in the United States of America,
North Mankato, Minnesota
112010
012011

 THIS BOOK CONTAINS AT LEAST 10% RECYCLED MATERIALS.

Editor: Chrös McDougall
Copy Editor: Susan M. Freese
Interior Design and Production: Craig Hinton
Cover Design: Craig Hinton

Photo Credits: Susan Walsh/AP Image, cover; Luis M. Alvarez/AP Image, 4; Nick Wass/AP Image, 7, 29; Winslow Townson/AP Image, 9; Jacques Boissinot/AP Image/The Canadian Press, 10, 13; Karl DeBlaker/AP Image, 14; Kevin Wolf/AP Image, 17; Gene J. Puskar/AP Image, 18; Greg Baker/AP Image, 20; Paul Chiasson /AP Image/The Canadian Press, 23; Ryan Remiorz/AP Image/The Canadian Press, 25; Julie Jacobson/AP Image, 26

Library of Congress Cataloging-in-Publication Data

McMahon, Dave.
  Alex Ovechkin : NHL superstar / by Dave McMahon.
    p. cm. — (Playmakers)
  ISBN 978-1-61714-750-0
  1. Ovechkin, Alexander, 1985—Juvenile literature. 2. Hockey players—United States—Biography—Juvenile literature. 3. Washington Capitals (Hockey team)—Juvenile literature. I. Title.
  GV848.5.O94M36 2011
  796.962092—dc22
  [B]
                                    2010046358

TABLE OF CONTENTS

Alex Ovechkin

CHAPTER 1

GROWING UP IN MOSCOW

Today, Alex Ovechkin is a National Hockey League (NHL) superstar. The powerful left winger won the Hart Memorial Trophy in 2007–08 and 2008–09. That award is given each year to the NHL's Most Valuable Player (MVP). Those who knew Ovechkin during his childhood in Moscow, Russia, were not at all surprised to see his success.

Alex comes from an athletic family. His father, Mikhail, was a top soccer player. His mother, Tatiana,

Alex Ovechkin is one of the NHL's biggest stars.

was one of the best women's basketball players in Russia's history. She even won gold medals playing basketball for the Soviet Union in the 1976 and 1980 Olympic Games.

Alex was only six years old in 1991 when the Soviet Union fell and the nation of Russia was formed. After that, Russian youngsters were exposed to many different cultures. American culture was one of Alex's favorites. In fact, Russia became so much like the United States that young Alex collected hockey trading cards with his father.

Alex's parents met through the Dynamo Sports Club in Moscow. The club was created in 1923. By 1971, it offered 45 different sports. They included soccer, basketball, volleyball, team handball, and ice hockey. Mikhail and Tatiana later passed on their love for Dynamo to their children.

Alex was born on September 17, 1985. He was the Ovechkins' third child. It didn't take him long to pick up his parents' interest in sports. Alex was only two years old when he became hooked on ice hockey. One day, he was in a toy store and picked up a toy hockey stick, a puck, and a helmet.

Alex (8) has loved playing hockey since he first picked up a stick at age two.

His mother told him to put down the toys so they could leave. But Alex didn't want to.

Hockey quickly became Alex's obsession. He would throw a tantrum if his parents tried to change channels while a hockey game was on TV. But he wasn't able to play on a youth hockey team for many years. His parents were too busy and didn't have time to take him to practices and games.

Alex was very upset when he saw how well his teammates played at his first youth hockey practice. He later told a *Washington Post* reporter that he was so mad that he said to his dad, "We must practice and get stronger, stronger."

That changed in 1992, when Alex was seven. He joined his first Dynamo youth team that year. Most of the other kids on the team had already been playing for a couple of years. Alex was concerned when the coach asked the players to skate backward figure eights. He didn't even know how to skate backward. But his coach quickly noticed his special talent.

Alex's parents were still very busy. So his older brother, Sergei, helped out. He made sure Alex was always able to get to and from his practices and games.

Tragedy struck three years later. Sergei died in a car crash. The family grieved for their loss. But they didn't let it ruin Alex's dream of playing hockey.

Alex's passion for the game has helped him become one of the best hockey players of his generation.

Alex Ovechkin

CHAPTER 2

MAKING HIS MARK

Alex Ovechkin continued to excel on the ice into his early teens. But there were no junior teams or leagues for him to play in after his youth career. So he began playing professional hockey when he was 16.

The Dynamo Sports Club was the perfect place for Alex to develop his skills. He played in 22 games for Dynamo during his first season in 2001–02. He scored two goals and had two assists.

Alex starred for Russia's youth national teams before coming to the NHL.

Alex was too young to enter the 2003 NHL Draft. But that did not stop the Florida Panthers from trying to select him. The Panthers selected Alex in the ninth round. They said that he was old enough to be drafted if leap years were accounted for. The NHL didn't agree.

The Russian national team soon noticed Alex. In 2002, he suited up for Russia in the Under-18 World Championship. Alex helped Russia win a silver medal by scoring 14 goals in eight games.

Alex was selected to play for Russia's junior national team in 2003. Juniors are age 20 or younger. His team competed in the World Junior Championship in Nova Scotia, Canada. That was when North American fans began learning about the 17-year-old star. Alex was a year younger than most of the players in the tournament. But he was Russia's team captain. He also scored six goals in six games as Russia won the gold medal.

The 2003 NHL Draft took place the following summer. Alex likely would have been selected early in the draft. However, he was not quite old enough to enter. His eighteenth birthday was just two days after the deadline.

Alex, *center*, and his teammates sing their national anthem after Russia won the 2003 World Junior Championship.

Alex went back for a third season with Dynamo in the Russian Super League. He was already one of the best players in Russia's top hockey league. Teams in the NHL could not wait for the chance to draft him.

Alex Ovechkin

CHAPTER 3

THE TOP PICK

Alex Ovechkin was too young to enter the 2003 NHL Draft. But if he had entered, many people thought he would have been the first pick. Some even thought he would have gone first in the 2002 draft. So it was pretty certain that Ovechkin would be picked first when he finally entered the draft in 2004.

The order in which NHL teams select players in the draft is based on a lottery. The Washington

The Washington Capitals selected Ovechkin first in the 2004 NHL Draft.

Capitals had only a one-in-seven chance of winning the top pick. But they got it! And of course, they selected Ovechkin.

Before Ovechkin suited up for the Capitals, he was named to Russia's national team. It was playing in the World Cup of Hockey. The tournament took place before the NHL season was set to begin. At age 19, Ovechkin was the youngest player in the tournament. But at 6 feet, 2 inches and 214 pounds, he fit right in with the older players. Even so, Russia lost in the quarterfinals.

> "He walked up to me and said, 'What do we do, Coach?' That's the way he is. He follows every direction. He does things superstars just don't do."
> —Washington Capitals coach Bruce Boudreau on meeting Ovechkin in the locker room for the first time, as told to the *New York Times*

Ovechkin was set to start playing in the NHL for the 2004–05 season. But that entire season was cancelled because of a dispute between the owners and the players. So Ovechkin played one more season with Dynamo Moscow.

Ovechkin was an immediate NHL star when he had more than 100 points in his rookie season.

The NHL picked up again in the next season. By then, Ovechkin had played three full seasons of pro hockey in Russia. It showed. His first NHL game was on October 5, 2005. The 20-year-old helped the Capitals beat the Columbus Blue Jackets 3–2. That first game was a preview of what was to come. Ovechkin showed the qualities he would soon be known for: strength, quickness, power, creativity, grit, and determination.

The arrivals of Ovechkin, *front,* and Sidney Crosby in the 2004–05 season excited NHL fans.

His charisma also showed. He liked being in the spotlight. He also scored two goals in the game.

Ovechkin didn't slow down. He scored at least one point in each of his first eight games. In 81 games that season, he had 52 goals and 54 assists. He finished third in the NHL in scoring.

Throughout his career, Ovechkin has been known for scoring incredible goals. His rookie year was no exception.

During a game against the Phoenix Coyotes, Ovechkin was sliding away from the goal on his back. But he was able to keep one hand on his stick. He used the tip of the stick to grab the puck and put it in the net. That amazing score is now known simply as "The Goal."

Hockey fans were excited to see Ovechkin shine in his first season. He was one of two young players to take the NHL by storm that year. The other was Sidney Crosby of the Pittsburgh Penguins.

Ovechkin and Sidney Crosby played against each other for the first time on November 22, 2005. Crosby had the edge. He had a goal and an assist in Pittsburgh's 5–4 victory over the Capitals. Ovechkin also had an assist but not a goal.

Both players were rookies in the 2005–06 season. But Ovechkin was the bigger star of the two. He scored more than 50 goals and got more than 100 points. That is a huge achievement for any player. Ovechkin won the Calder Trophy as the NHL's Rookie of the Year.

Alex Ovechkin

CHAPTER 4

BECOMING A STAR

A lex Ovechkin was enjoying his rookie season in the NHL when he had the chance to follow another dream. He was named to the Russian hockey team that would compete in the 2006 Olympic Winter Games. His mother had been an Olympic gold medalist. He now had a chance to match her achievement.

Ovechkin played well at the Olympics. He scored five goals in Team Russia's eight games. One of those

Anton Volchenkov lifted Ovechkin into the air after Ovechkin scored a goal during the 2006 Olympics.

goals was the game winner against Canada in the quarterfinals. But Russia lost in the semifinals. Then the team lost the game for the bronze medal to the Czech Republic.

Even President Barack Obama is glad that Ovechkin chose to play hockey in the NHL. Speaking at a graduation ceremony in Moscow in July 2009, Obama said, "As a resident of Washington DC, I continue to benefit from the contributions of Russians—specifically, from Alexander Ovechkin. We're very pleased to have him in Washington DC."

Ovechkin continued his success during his second NHL season. The young star scored 46 goals and added 46 assists for 92 points. And his opponents feared his hard checks. However, Ovechkin often struggled on defense. He posted a team-worst rating of minus-19. That meant that the Capitals' opponents scored 19 more goals than the Capitals did when Ovechkin was on the ice.

Ovechkin worked hard to improve his defensive play, and he succeeded. He had a plus-28 rating during the 2007–08 season. That was the seventh-best rating in the league. He also

Ovechkin worked hard to improve his defense for the 2007–08 NHL season.

scored 65 goals and had 47 assists for 112 points. The Capitals made the playoffs for the first time since Ovechkin joined the team. They lost in the first round. But it was still a successful season for Ovechkin.

The 22-year-old led the NHL in many offensive statistics and won four major awards. He won the Maurice "Rocket" Richard Trophy for scoring the most goals. He also won the

> **A Gold Medal**
>
> In 2008, Ovechkin and his Russian team beat Canada 5–4 in overtime to win the World Championship. The Washington Capitals left winger had two assists in the gold medal game.

Art Ross Trophy for earning the most points. Ovechkin won the Lester B. Pearson Award after being selected as the league's MVP by his fellow players. And he won the Hart Memorial Trophy after being selected as MVP by the media.

Ovechkin led the league in scoring again during the next season, in 2008–09. He had 56 goals, and his 110 total points was second in the NHL. In the playoffs, he helped the Capitals beat the New York Rangers in the first round. Ovechkin had a hat trick in a second-round game against the Pittsburgh Penguins. But the team fell short of winning the Stanley Cup again. Ovechkin ended the season by scoring 21 points in 14 playoff games. But the Capitals lost to the Penguins in seven games.

It was another disappointing ending to an NHL season. However, Ovechkin showed that he was one of the game's

Ovechkin posed with the Hart Memorial Trophy, the Lester B. Pearson Trophy, and the Maurice Richard Trophy in 2009.

best-ever players. He won the Hart Memorial Trophy again that season. That put in him the record books next to Wayne Gretzky. Gretzky was the last hockey player who wasn't a goaltender to win back-to-back Hart Trophies. He won it every year from 1980 to 1987.

Alex Ovechkin

CHAPTER 5

FACING CHALLENGES

Alex Ovechkin missed only four games during his first four NHL seasons. Then he missed 10 games during the 2009–10 season. Some of his absences were due to injury and others to suspension. But the left winger still ended up with 109 points. His 59 assists that season were a career high. His plus-45 rating was second best in the league.

After the season, fellow players once again voted Ovechkin as the league MVP. This was the third

The 2010 Olympics were not very memorable for Ovechkin and Team Russia.

straight year that he won the Ted Lindsay Award (formerly the Lester B. Pearson Award).

Ovechkin had established himself as a top-level player by the end of his fifth regular season. But the 2009–10 season ended in disappointment for the Capitals star. The frustration began at the Olympics that February.

Ovechkin was expected to star as his Russian team made a run for the gold medal. Many fans hoped to see Ovechkin's Team Russia and Sidney Crosby's Team Canada meet in the gold-medal game. Instead, the two teams met in the quarterfinals. Ovechkin was held scoreless as Russia lost 7–3.

Ovechkin had a chance to redeem himself in the NHL's Stanley Cup playoffs. He was the biggest star on a team full of talented players. The Capitals had the best record in the NHL. But they lost to the eighth-ranked Montreal Canadiens in the first round of the playoffs.

Alex Ovechkin is expected to be an NHL star for many years to come.

The 2009–10 season was difficult for Ovechkin. But the big left-winger didn't seem to be slowing down. At the start of the 2010–11 NHL season, he was just 25 years old. He had also signed to play for the Capitals for a long time. With a long career ahead of him, Alex Ovechkin will have many more opportunities to lift the Stanley Cup and to kiss an Olympic gold medal.

FUN FACTS AND QUOTES

- As a 17-year-old, Alex Ovechkin was studying to be a border guard at the Moscow Military Institute while playing for Dynamo Moscow in the Russian pro league. If he had not become a hockey player, he would have had a job checking passports at a city on the Russian border.

- Ovechkin's mother, Tatiana, and his father, Mikhail, never sit next to each other when they watch his games. When asked by a reporter why they don't sit together, Tatiana said, "Superstition."

- Following Ovechkin's rookie season with the Capitals, he was selected to throw out the ceremonial first pitch at the Washington Nationals professional baseball game. Until that day, he had never thrown a baseball or swung a bat. The *Washington Post* reported that "his only experience of the game was playing electronic baseball on his PlayStation as a boy growing up in Moscow."

- Ovechkin gives tickets to a different group of underprivileged children for each home game at the Verizon Center. "I think for kids, it's very important when people take care of them," he told a reporter for the *New York Times*. "I want to give people a chance to see what [hockey is] because if they don't know what's going on, they can't come to the game and see us."

WEB LINKS

To learn more about Alex Ovechkin, visit ABDO Publishing Company online at **www.abdopublishing.com**. Web sites about Ovechkin are featured on our Book Links page. These links are routinely monitored and updated to provide the most current information available.

GLOSSARY

assist
A pass that leads directly to a goal.

charisma
Personal charm or appeal.

check
Using physical contact to keep an opposing player out of the play.

culture
The shared beliefs and values of a group.

draft
A system in which teams select new players.

hat trick
The act of scoring three goals in a hockey game.

left winger
A forward on a hockey team who plays primarily on the left side of the rink.

lottery
A system that selects a winner by chance.

media
Forms of communication such as newspapers and magazines, radio and television, and Web sites.

passport
An official document issued by the government of a country to one of its citizens that proves his or her identity and authorizes him or her to travel to and from other countries.

points
Goals or assists.

rookie
A first-year player in the NHL.

superstition
A belief that isn't based on reason or knowledge.

INDEX

FURTHER RESOURCES

Cox, Damien, and Gare Joyce. *The Ovechkin Project: A Behind-the-Scenes Look at Hockey's Most Dangerous Player.* Hoboken, NJ: Wiley, 2010.

Lansdell, Geoffrey. *Alexander Ovechkin.* Montreal, Quebec: OverTime Books, 2009.

Leonetti, Mike. *Hockey Now!* 5th ed. Buffalo, NY: Firefly Books, 2008.